ALL ABOUT

THE

12 DISCIPLES

by Dave Snyder
Illustrated by Noah Chambers

ALL ABOUT: THE 12 DISCIPLES

All rights reserved. No part of this book may be reproduced or transmitted in any form or by any means, electronic or mechanical, including photocopying and recording, or by any informational storage and retrieval system, without permission in writing from the publisher.

Unless otherwise noted, all Scripture quotations are taken from the HCSB®, Copyright © 1999, 2000, 2002, 2003, 2009 by Holman Bible Publishers. Used by permission. HCSB® is a federally registered trademark of Holman Bible Publishers.

ISBN: 9781790808076

Text copyright © 2019 by David Snyder.
Illustrations copyright © 2019 by Noah Chambers. All rights reserved.

Bubba Books Publishing

ALL ABOUT THE 12 DISCIPLES

Introduction	5
CHAPTER 1	10
WHO WERE THE TWELVE	
CHAPTER 2	20
CHOOSING THE TWELVE	
CHAPTER 3	30
LIFE WITH JESUS	
CHAPTER 4	38
BECOMING APOSTLES	
CHAPTER 5	45
THE CRUCIFIXION	
Chapter 6	55
THE RESURRECTION	
Chapter 7	61
ACTS OF THE APOSTLES	
Chapter 8	73
THE UTTERMOST PARTS OF THE EARTH	
Bibliography	96

Introduction

Peter and John stood before the Jewish leaders, knowing they could be facing a death penalty. These same leaders had handed Jesus over to the Romans for crucifixion just a few weeks ago. Now His disciples were turning the city upside down, preaching about Jesus, and performing miracles.

Earlier that morning, Peter and John had been walking to the Temple in Jerusalem for the time of prayer. Before they entered, a beggar, paralyzed from birth, stopped them. Every day his friends would pick him up and take him where he could sit and beg. The beggar sat with his hand stretched out toward them.

Peter looked him in the eye and told him he had no money. The man dropped his eyes to the ground in disappointment. But then Peter said something that changed the man forever, "what I have, I give to you: In the name of Jesus Christ the Nazarene, get up and walk!!"[1]

Peter took his hand and helped the man stand up. The man was surprised as he stood and felt his legs move for the first time in his life. He walked and jumped as he praised God!

The word spread like wildfire. People had seen this man sitting in the same place for years. Now they crowded around him to see the miracle. Peter told the crowd, Jesus had made the man whole. He said they should put their faith in Jesus.

---

[1] Acts 3:6

As he spoke, the Jewish leaders came and arrested Peter and John. The leaders thought they had stopped Jesus when they had Him crucified. Then they heard He had risen from the dead. And now His disciples were preaching in His name. The city was in an uproar and the leaders were furious.

They confronted Peter and John and commanded them to stop preaching in the name of Jesus.

Peter looked at them and said, "Whether it's right in the sight of God for us to listen to you rather than to God, you decide; for we are unable to stop speaking about what we have seen and heard."[2]

The leaders threw up their hands. They didn't know how to stop them. They made this observation about the Apostles: "When they observed the boldness of Peter and John and realized that they were uneducated and untrained men, they were amazed and recognized that they had been with Jesus."[3]

This statement is true of all the Apostles. They were ordinary men who met an extraordinary Savior, and He changed them forever. Jesus entrusted these men to carry His Gospel to the ends of the earth.

---

[2] Acts 4:19

[3] Acts 4:13

Jesus chose twelve men and shared His life with them. They were an unlikely group, but the thing that would define them for the rest of their lives was that they had been with Jesus.

CHAPTER 1
WHO WERE THE TWELVE

Jesus knew His time on earth would be brief, and the men He chose would take the message of the Gospel to the world. But who were these men who gave up everything to follow Jesus?

The Bible tells us a few details about some disciples, but others only get a passing mention. Here is what we know about them.

Most of the Apostles lived in Galilee, in the northern part of Israel. The town of Nazareth, where Jesus grew up, is also in Galilee. At

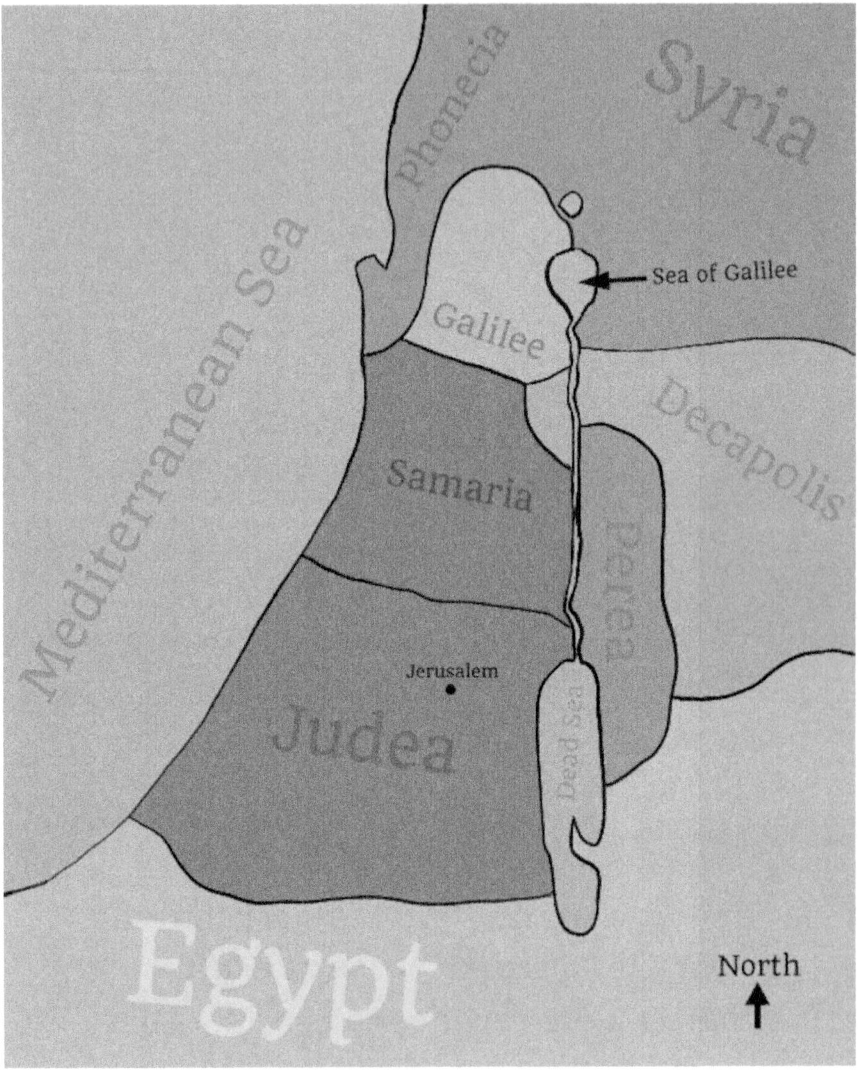
Syria
Phonecia
Mediterranean Sea
Sea of Galilee
Galilee
Decapolis
Samaria
Perea
Jerusalem
Judea
Dead Sea
Egypt
North

least four disciples were fishermen who worked on the Sea of Galilee, like Peter and his brother Andrew. And another set of brothers, James and John, the sons of Zebedee. Their father Zebedee owned the fishing business, and both sets of brothers probably worked for him.

The way people fish on the Sea of Galilee hasn't changed much in 2,000 years. Commercial fishermen stretch long nets between two boats. The nets are big enough to touch the bottom of the lake. One boat moves in a circle until it comes to the other end of the net. People in boats pull the nets up, and anything swimming in the area gets caught.

Other disciples might have been fishermen too, but not all of them, like Matthew, the tax collector.

A tax collector was a despised man. People didn't like them because they worked for the Roman state. If you were Jewish, people expected you to help the Jews, not Rome.

The Romans introduced all kinds of taxes, like sales tax, trade tax, and land tax. They had taxes for using the roads, taxes for using bridges, taxes for crossing rivers, and using harbors. If you could think of it, they taxed it.

Tax collectors could stop anyone and force them to pay a tax. They had the right to inspect people and could even have them strip off their clothes to be sure they weren't smuggling anything that should be taxed. The tax collectors were notorious for collecting extra money from the people to put in their own pockets. This behavior earned them a reputation as some of the worst people in society. But Jesus chose one of these men to be His disciple.

Jesus faced criticism for spending time with tax collectors and sinners. But He shrugged it off, saying, it wasn't the healthy who needed a doctor but the sick. His mission was to save lost people, like Matthew, and he was a changed person when he met Jesus.

Some of the disciples came from a group known as the Zealots. The Zealots wanted to see Israel return to its former glory and get the Romans out of the country. Many of them were very violent. They would start riots and even murder anyone loyal to Rome. But Jesus chose people from this group to follow Him.

One of those men was Simon the Zealot. He earned the title because of his connection with that group before he met Jesus. Some think several of the disciples were also members of this group, including Judas (also called Thaddeus), Judas Iscariot, and even James, the son of Alphaeus.

We might find it surprising that Jesus would choose people like Matthew and Simon to be his disciples. But Jesus chose these men for a reason. He wasn't concerned with who they were but who they would become.

When God chose David to be the King of Israel, He told the Prophet Samuel that He doesn't look at the outside but at the heart of a man. Jesus saw something in these men others couldn't. He does the same with us. We might look in the mirror and not see anything special, but God looks into our hearts and makes plans for us that are bigger than we are.

There may have been another set of brothers in the group. You already know Peter and Andrew were brothers, and so were James and John. The other set of brothers was Matthew and the other James. The Bible doesn't specifically call them brothers, but they are both called 'the son of Alphaeus.' Maybe it was a coincidence they both had a father with the same name. But most likely, they were brothers.

The only disciple who wasn't from Galilee was Judas Iscariot, the disciple who betrayed Jesus. The name Iscariot means he was from a place called Kerioth in Judea. We don't know much about Judas' background. Some think he was part of the same group of Zealots as Simon. If this is true, it might explain why he betrayed Jesus. He wanted to force Jesus into action and make Him the King. When he learned they would crucify Jesus, he tried to undo his betrayal by trying to give the money back, but it was too late.

In the Gospels, we find different names for some of the Apostles. The reason for that is that people didn't use last names the way they do today, so to set people apart, they chose nicknames or secondary names. They might have one name at home, but at school or work, everyone called them by another name like Simon Peter. His name was Simon, but Jesus called him Peter.

Most people spoke Greek as well as their native language. So they had Greek versions of their names too. The Greek translation of Peter was Cephas, and Thomas was Didymus. Thomas's name was a nickname since it means 'twin.' Some people think he was a relative of Jesus and looked like Him, so they called him the 'twin' of Jesus. It was even possible that Thomas was a carpenter like Jesus. Matthew had another name. In the book of Mark, he is called Levi.

All these different names can be confusing. When Matthew, Mark, Luke, and John each recorded their Gospels, they used different names for a few of the disciples. That means in one Gospel, we might read a story about Nathanael. But in another Gospel, it doesn't even mention Nathanael in his list. That is because they chose to use one of his other names.

Here are the 12 Apostles.

1. **Simon** also called **Peter**

2. **Andrew**

3. **James** (the brother of John) Jesus called James and his brother John the *'Sons of Thunder.'*

4. **John**

5. **Philip**

6. **Nathanael**, they also called him **Bartholomew**. '*Bar*' means 'son of' in Hebrew. It means he was the 'son of Tolmai.'

7. **Matthew** sometimes called **Levi**

8. **Thomas** or **Didymus**. Thomas is Hebrew for 'twin.' Didymus is the Greek version of his name.

9. **James**, *the son of Alphaeus*

10. **Simon**, the Zealot

11. **Thaddeus** is also known as **Judas**, the brother of James. He might have dropped the

name Judas so people wouldn't confuse him with Judas Iscariot.

12. **Judas Iscariot**

CHAPTER 2
CHOOSING THE TWELVE

Andrew & Peter

Andrew was the first disciple to follow Jesus. He was a fisherman along with his brother Simon. Andrew had been a disciple of John the Baptist and was there when John baptized Jesus. He heard John's testimony about Jesus and saw with his own eyes as the Holy Spirit came down on him. Then he heard God's voice from heaven, "This is my beloved Son. I take delight in Him."[1]

---

[1] Matthew 3:17

The next day Andrew noticed Jesus passing by and followed Him. The first thing he did was get his brother Simon and take him to Jesus. When Jesus saw Simon, He called him by his proper name, Simon, son of Jonah. He told him his name would be Cephas or Peter from then on. Cephas was the Greek version of Peter, but both names mean, 'a stone.'

Jesus was telling Peter he would be a different person from that point on. His father's name was Jonah, which means dove. Jesus might have been saying that until then, he was a man who wasn't stable but floated through life like a bird. But now he would be Peter, which means rock. Jesus would turn him into a strong, steady man. But it would take time for Peter to live up to that name.

Philip & Nathanael

When Philip met Jesus, he was so excited he ran home and found his friend, Nathanael.

Nathanael was sitting next to his house under a fig tree. At that time, most people planted fig trees near their homes. They liked the fruit, but the tree also gave them privacy. If you wanted to be alone, all you had to do was duck under the canopy of the fig tree. It would provide shade and privacy to pray or take a nap. Philip pulled back the branches and stuck his head inside.

"'We have found the One Moses wrote about in the Law (and so did the prophets): Jesus the son of Joseph, from Nazareth!'

'Can anything good come out of Nazareth?' Nathanael asked him."

Together the two of them went to meet Jesus. When Jesus looked at Nathanael, He could peer inside him as Andrew did with the fig tree. "Here is a true Israelite; no deceit is in him."

Nathanael had never met Jesus and asked Him how He knew him.

"Before Philip called you when you were under the fig tree, I saw you," Jesus answered.

That was enough to convince Nathanael. He told Jesus he believed He was the Son of God.

Jesus said to him, "Do you believe only because I told you I saw you under the fig tree? You will see greater things than this."[2]

Matthew

Matthew was sitting in his tax collectors booth when Jesus called him. Without a second thought, he left it all behind and followed Jesus. Matthew walked away from his job and the financial security that came with it. He couldn't believe it that Jesus would want someone like him. The other disciples could relate to that feeling. They weren't leaders in their communities. They were uneducated, flawed, ordinary men, but Jesus called them.

The Gospel of Luke goes into more detail about how Peter came to follow Jesus. Maybe a day or two had passed since his first encounter with Jesus. He had been out fishing all night and hadn't caught a thing. He pulled

---

[2] John 1:43-51

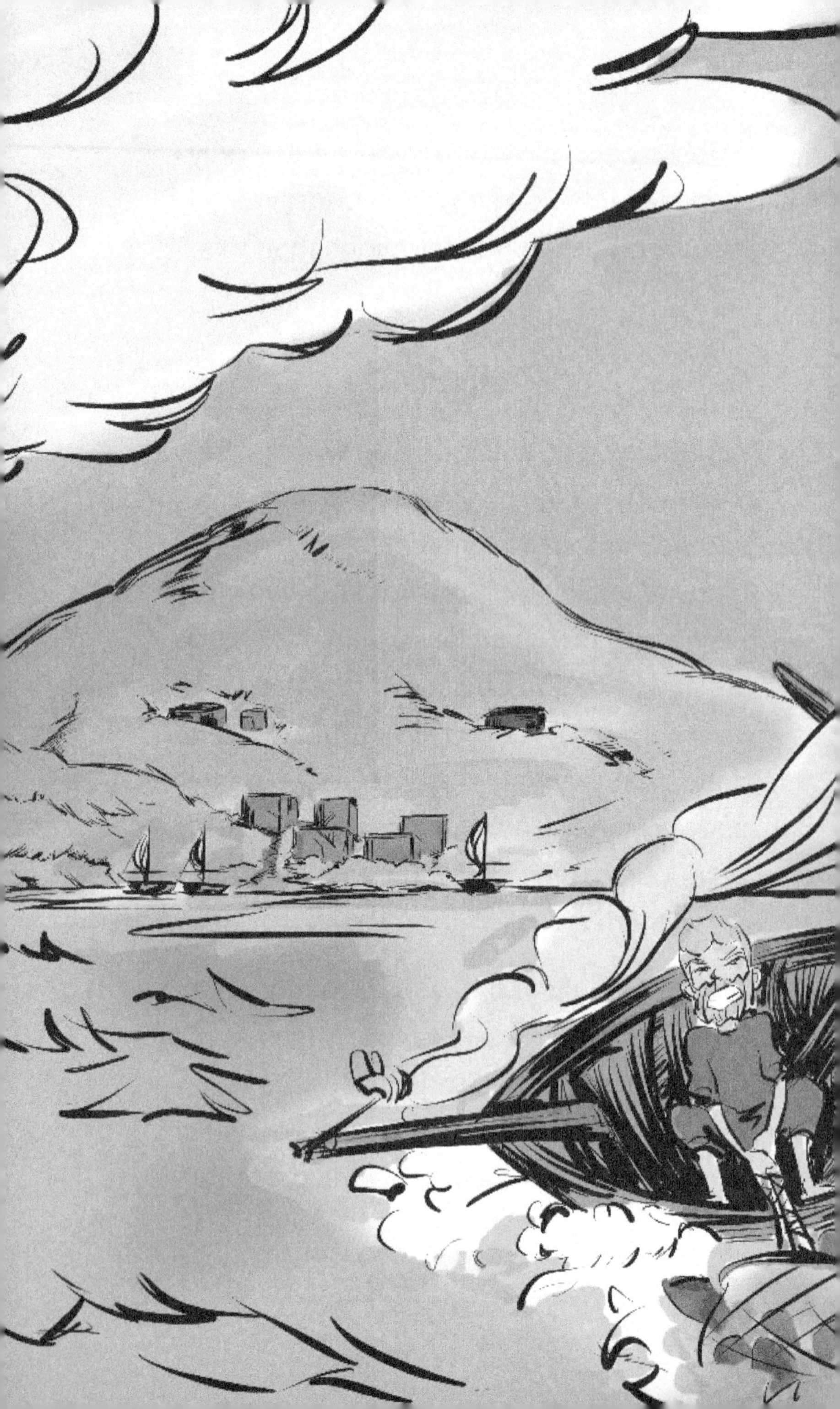

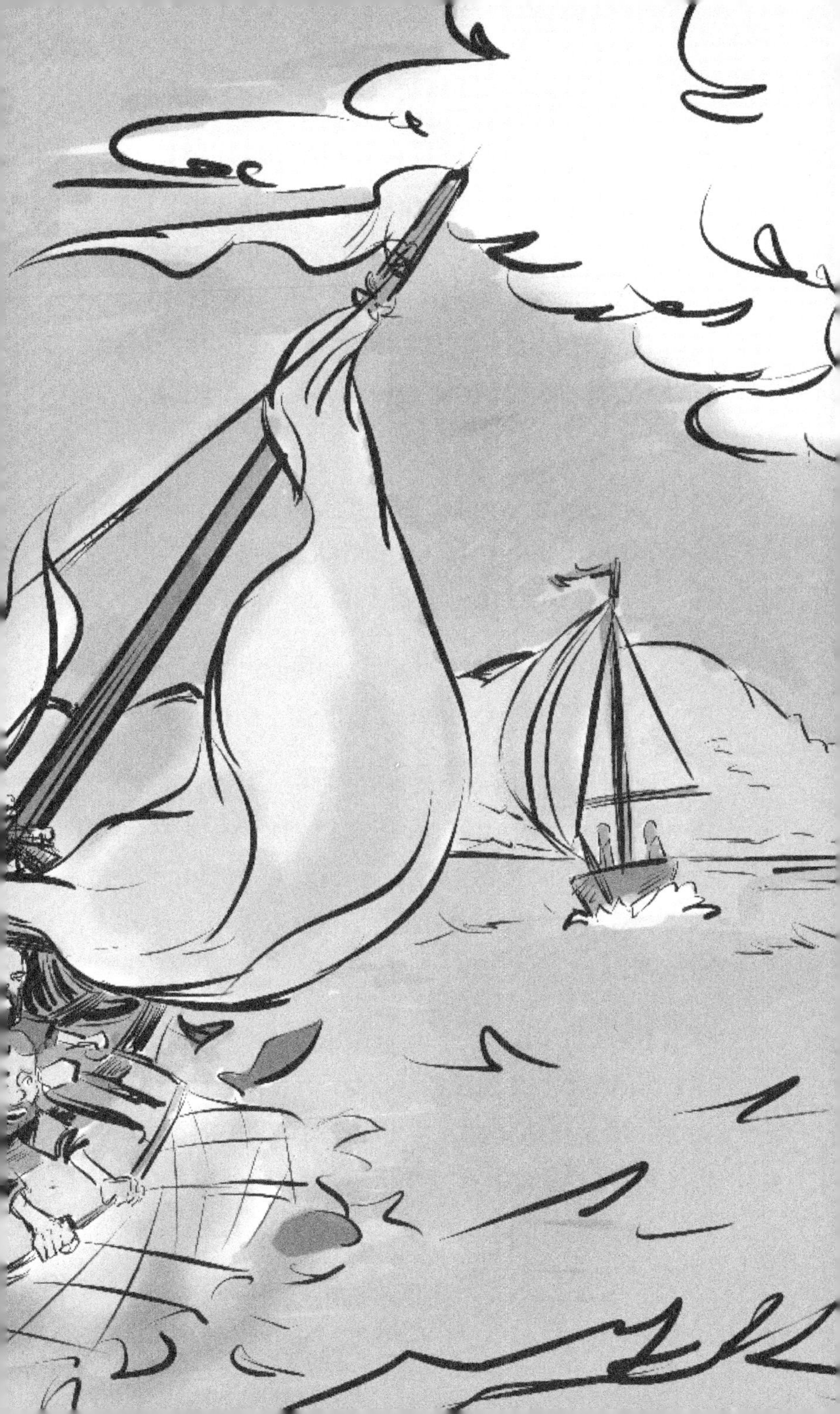

his boat up to the shore and began the long process of washing and drying the nets. Then he noticed a crowd gathering on the beach. Peter wondered what was going on. Then Jesus approached him and asked to use his boat as a platform to speak. Peter quickly agreed.

Peter sat in the boat, listening but tired from a night of fishing. After a while, Jesus dismissed the crowd and turned to Peter.

"Let's head out in deep water and catch some fish," Jesus said.

Peter hesitated. He was tired. They had already washed the nets, and above all, it wasn't the time of day to catch fish. But Peter didn't want to insult Jesus, so he nodded in agreement.

It took time, but soon Peter had the boat out and the net ready. As soon as he dropped the nets in the water, it filled up with fish. The fish filled the net and made it so heavy that Peter couldn't pull it up. James and John arrived in another boat to help haul the fish onboard. As they struggled with the nets, the weight of the incredible catch of fish brought both boats dangerously close to sinking. Peter trembled in fear when he saw the catch of fish. It wasn't natural.

Peter begged Jesus to go away from him, with tears running down his face. He told Jesus he is a sinful man. He didn't feel worthy of being near Jesus.

Jesus tells him not to be afraid. From that moment on, he would be catching people.

James & John

James and John watched all these things, along with Peter and Andrew. Jesus called to each of them, "Come follow me." It was the call He gave to all His disciples. The choice was theirs. They could stay and continue with life as usual or step out into the most excellent adventure of their lives. None of them hesitated. They left their nets there and followed Jesus. But they weren't just leaving nets. They were also leaving jobs and families. Life as they knew it would never be the same.

CHAPTER 3
LIFE WITH JESUS

Jesus called the twelve, and they followed Him even though they did not understand what was in store. Others followed Him and were called disciples, but Jesus chose the twelve to be part of an intimate circle.

Some of them were following Him because they believed He was the Messiah, but they didn't understand what that meant. They assumed the Messiah was coming to restore Israel and set up a kingdom on this earth. Jesus wasn't what they were expecting, but they followed Him with anticipation.

The more they followed Him, the more the anticipation grew. The disciples received an invitation to a wedding soon after they began to follow Jesus. They felt honored to attend alongside Jesus, but they weren't expecting what happened that day.

At that time, weddings lasted for several days as people celebrated with the bride and groom. On the final day of the wedding, the wine ran out. It would embarrass the bride and groom and would mean the party would end early. Jesus didn't seem too concerned until His mother asked Him to do something.

He gave instructions to fill up large jars with water. Someone handed a cup to the man in charge of the wedding. He took a sip, and his eyes lit up. He took a bigger drink, then went and patted the groom on the back. He told him most people served the best wine first, but he saved the best for last. Neither man realized just a few moments ago the wine had been water. But the disciples knew.

The disciples put their faith in Him at that moment. But they still didn't understand His mission. Jesus would explain to them over the next several years, how He would suffer and die on the cross for the sin of the world. But that didn't fit with their ideas. They thought the Messiah was coming to rule the world.

The disciples witnessed incredible miracles while they were with Jesus. Like the time Jesus was teaching in a house. He suddenly had to stop mid-sermon because of noise on the roof. Everyone looked up and watched as a hole appeared, and bits of the ceiling fell. Then a mat was lowered into the room with ropes. A paralyzed man lay on the mat. When his friends couldn't get him inside to see Jesus, they had to get creative.

Jesus told him right there that He had forgiven his sins. The crowd gasped. Who did Jesus think He was to forgive sins? Only God could do that. But then Jesus said, "so you may know that the Son of Man has authority on earth to forgive sins… I tell you: Get up, pick up your mat, and go home."[1] And the man did.

Once Jesus saw a blind man and felt sorry for him, so He walked up to him, spit on the ground and made mud. He rubbed it on the man's eyes and told him to go wash it off. When the man did, he could see.

The disciples watched all these things with amazement and wonder. They would remember these events for the rest of their

---

[1] Luke 5:24

lives, and they would tell everyone they met about the things Jesus did. Some miracles Jesus performed got a lot of attention. The disciples would never forget when the leader of the synagogue came and asked Jesus to heal his sick daughter.

Jesus went with the man, but on the way, someone came and said his daughter had already died. Jesus encouraged him not to be afraid but to believe. They kept walking toward the house, and the disciples watched as the man bravely fought back the tears.

When they got to the house, they noticed people crying and playing sad music. That is how people showed they cared when someone died. The whole village would turn up and mourn. Jesus asked them why they were making a scene? He told them the girl wasn't dead. He said she was only sleeping. The crowd laughed at Jesus! It was apparent to them the girl was a corpse. But Jesus sent them all outside. He told the girl, "Get up!" And the girl sat up. That got people talking.

The disciples lived in a constant state of wonder with Jesus. Just when they thought they had seen it all, He would surprise them again. One day Jesus was teaching. When He finished, He sent His disciples out across the lake in a boat. But He stayed and prayed half the night and then decided to cross the lake too. No boats were around, so Jesus walked on top of the lake! It was the middle of the night when Jesus got to where the disciples were. They had been rowing for hours but were struggling to cross the lake.

The disciples shook with fear when they saw Jesus coming toward them. It looked like a ghost, but Jesus told them to calm down, it was only Him.

Peter wasn't so sure. He asked Jesus if it was really Him, to let him come out on the water to meet Him.

Jesus responded with one word, "Come."

Peter stepped out, testing the water. To his surprise, he didn't sink. He set his other foot out and can't believe he is walking on water. After a few steps, he noticed the waves and fear took hold of his heart. Suddenly he was sinking. He cried out for Jesus to save Him. Jesus ran to him and pulled him out of the water.

"You of little faith, why did you doubt?"[2] Jesus asks him.

It was part of Jesus' mission to lead people from a place of doubt and fear to faith. Faith means believing God and trusting Him. Jesus scolded His disciples several times for not having faith. Once a storm popped up while they were crossing the lake. This group was familiar with the sea, and they knew a bad storm when they saw one. Their lives were in danger, they panicked, but when they looked for Jesus, they found Him sleeping in the back of the boat. The disciples woke Him up. They asked if He even cared they were all about to die.

---

[2] Matthew 14:31

Jesus got up and told the storm, "Silence! Be still!"[3] At that instant, the waves turned smooth as glass, and the wind stopped blowing. Jesus scolded the disciples again for not having faith. But they sat shaking their heads. Even a storm obeyed Jesus.

In the time they were with Jesus, they watched Him heal the sick, raise the dead, cure diseases, walk on water, calm a storm, and feed five thousand people with a little boy's lunch. They saw Jesus do so many incredible things that the disciple John said if he tried to write everything down, the entire world couldn't hold all the books he would fill up.

---

[3] Mark 4:39

CHAPTER 4
BECOMING APOSTLES

Jesus took these twelve men called disciples and trained them to be Apostles. A disciple means they followed a teacher, but when Jesus called them Apostles, it means He was sending them with His authority. Like a representative or an ambassador. Jesus was launching the disciples to preach and do what He had been doing.

Parables

When Jesus spoke in public, He used parables. A parable is a story that teaches a point. People heard Him teach, but they didn't always understand what He was saying. But Jesus explained everything to His disciples.

In His parables, Jesus taught truths about the kingdom of heaven, what it was like, and how to live. The disciples weren't afraid to ask questions. When they didn't know the right way to pray, they asked Jesus to teach them. He didn't hold back anything from them. He was teaching and preparing His disciples for what they would need one day. It was vital for them to know how to live and be able to teach others after He had gone back to the Father.

When Jesus spoke a parable, the disciples would always ask later what He meant. Sometimes He was surprised they didn't understand a parable. But He explained everything and answered their questions.

Here is an example of the type of parables Jesus taught. It is called the Parable of the Lost Sheep.

What man among you who has 100 sheep and loses one of them, does not leave the 99 in the open field and go after the lost one until he finds it? When he has found it, he joyfully puts it on his shoulders, and coming home, he calls his friends and neighbors together, saying to them, 'Rejoice with me, because I have found my lost sheep!'... In the same way, there will be more joy in heaven over one sinner who repents than over 99 righteous people who don't need repentance.[1]

---

[1] Luke 15:4-7

Jesus wanted His disciples to change their thinking and see life and people the way He did. He wanted them to put into practice what they had been learning by going out on their own. He gave them instructions as He sent them out, "As you go, announce this: 'The kingdom of heaven has come near.' Heal the sick, raise the dead, cleanse those with skin diseases, drive out demons."[2]

The disciples must have been nervous and scared at first. They had seen Jesus do these things, but He was Jesus! Did He really expect them to do miracles and preach the way He did? But they understood Jesus was giving them His authority. He wanted them to be His ambassadors. Jesus warned them that people would treat them the same way they treated Him, which wasn't always good. Once a mob tried to push Him off a cliff, another time, they attempted to stone him to death.

But Jesus knew His disciples would need to learn to do what He had been doing. Soon, Jesus would be with God, and it would be up

---

[2] Matthew 10:7-8

to them to keep preaching and doing the works that Jesus did.

The Three

The disciples got to see everything Jesus did, but He chose three of His disciples to share special times. These three were Peter, James and his brother John. Remember these three were fishermen and worked together in the same fishing business. Jesus gave James and John the nickname, 'Sons of Thunder'. They must have been exciting boisterous men. They might have earned their nickname one day when a village refused to let Jesus enter. James and John wanted to call down fire from heaven and destroy the town. But Jesus told them He came to save people, not destroy them.

One significant moment these three shared with Jesus happened when He invited them to come up on top of a mountain with Him. While they were on the mountain, something incredible happened. Jesus started glowing! His clothes became bright white, and right before their eyes Elijah and Moses appeared and spoke to Jesus! It must have felt like a dream to the three disciples. Then a voice came from heaven. It said, "This is my beloved Son. I take delight in Him. Listen to Him."[3]

Then, Elijah and Moses disappeared and was back to normal. The disciples were shocked at what had just happened. Jesus told them not to tell anyone about it until He had risen from the dead. The disciples wondered what Jesus was getting at. What did rising from the dead mean? They must have thought He was speaking in a parable, but they would find out soon.

These three accompanied Jesus during the most stressful moment in His life. He was about to be betrayed by one of His disciples. He had gone to a garden to pray. He told the rest of the disciples to wait in one part of the garden, but He asked the three to come with Him further and pray, but Peter, James, and John kept falling asleep. Three times Jesus

---

[3] Matthew 17:5

woke them up. They didn't know what was about to happen. If they did, they would have stayed awake.

CHAPTER 5
THE CRUCIFIXION

The most momentous event in human history was about to take place, and the disciples had a front-row seat. It was a scary and uncertain time for them. Jesus explained He was going to the cross to suffer and die, but He would rise from the dead. But they didn't understand what He was saying.

The night Jesus was betrayed, He shared an intimate moment with His disciples. It was a special Jewish holiday called Passover. During the Passover meal, Jesus did something that surprised everyone. He took a

Passover

Passover is one of the most important holidays to the Jewish people because it celebrates their exodus from Egypt. During this time, they reflect on the conditions they lived in and how God brought them out with miracles. For eight days, they only eat bread without yeast, called matzah.

Jewish people celebrate Passover with a feast. During the feast, they remember the first Passover. On that night, they made their meals in a hurry, with everything ready for the long journey out of Egypt. God instructed them to kill a lamb and wipe the blood on their door. During the night, the Destroyer came and killed all the firstborn sons of the Egyptians, but things were different for God's people. When the Destroyer saw the blood, he passed over that house.

It was during the Passover meal that Jesus took the cup of wine and told His disciples it represented His blood. Jesus was connecting Himself with the Passover lamb. He was going to the cross to give His life for the world. His blood on our lives saves us from death and makes us right with God.

towel and a bucket of water, bent down, and washed the disciples' feet. Their mouths dropped open in shock. Washing feet was a job for a servant or young person, but not Jesus.

The disciples were confused, but only Peter dared to protest. He told Jesus He would never wash his feet!

Jesus told him he might not understand what He was doing, but one day he would. So Jesus washed all the disciples' feet, even Judas. Judas was the disciple who would betray Him that same night, but Jesus washed his feet along with the others. He told them He was giving them an example. Just like Jesus washed their feet, they should wash one another's feet too. Jesus wanted them to serve and care for one another as He served them.

Then Jesus sat down and shared a meal with the twelve. During the meal, He broke the bread and passed a piece to each of them and told them it represented His body that was going to be broken for them. Then He handed them a cup of wine and told them to drink it because it represented His blood that would be shed.

During the meal Jesus announced that one of the disciples would betray Him. The twelve looked at each other, wondering who it was. Jesus told them it was the one that He would hand His bread to. Then He gave the bread to Judas. Immediately Judas left and made a deal with the religious leaders. In exchange for betraying Jesus, they gave him thirty pieces of silver.

After Judas left, Jesus told the disciples He was about to lay down His life for them, and they would all run away. Peter spoke up. He said even if everyone else left, he never would.

Jesus looked told him that before the rooster crowed twice, he would deny him three times.

The disciples left that meal feeling sad and confused. They wondered if they would really run away from Jesus.

They spent the next few hours in an olive grove called the Garden of Gethsemane at the Mount of Olives. It was there that the disciples slept while Jesus prayed. Jesus prayed, "My Father! If it is possible, let this cup pass from Me. Yet not as I will, but as You will." He didn't want to go to the cross, but He knew it was the only way. He was in such agony that His sweat was like drops of blood.

Jesus finally prayed that the Father's will would be done. Then He got up from praying and woke Peter, James, and John. He told them the time had come.

They walked a short distance and found a crowd of soldiers with swords and torches. Then Judas approached Jesus and kissed Him on the cheek. The group fell into chaos. Peter took a sword and swung wildly at a soldier; he connected and sliced the man's ear clean off.

Jesus raised His hand and told him to put the sword away. "do you think that I cannot call on My Father, and He will provide Me at once with more than 12 legions of angels?"[1] But Jesus understood He had to go to the cross. He picked up the ear, put it back on the man's head, and healed him. The soldiers grabbed Jesus, and all the disciples turned and ran away, terrified. They were afraid the soldiers would arrest them too.

When Judas learned they were going to crucify Jesus, it upset him. He didn't want Jesus to die. He might have considered Jesus too passive and thought he could force him to step up and become the king. He tried to return the money, hoping to get Jesus released, but it was too late. Judas went out that night and took his own life.

The religious leaders turned Jesus over to the Romans, who would crucify Him. Most of the disciples were hiding. They were staying far away from everything, except for John and Peter. John had friends in the High Priest's house, maybe because of his father's fishing business, and could get inside where Jesus

---

[1] Matthew 26:53

was standing trial. He even got Peter through the gate, but he had to stay outside with the servants and soldiers.

Peter stood by a fire, keeping himself warm when he noticed people eyeing him suspiciously. He knew it would be dangerous if anyone discovered he was a disciple. He might face the same punishment as Jesus. A slave girl was there at the fire and accused him, "You were with Jesus the Galilean too."

"I don't know what you're talking about!" Peter told her.

Someone else recognized him. "This man was with Jesus the Nazarene!"[2]

Peter denied it again. Somewhere a rooster crowed.

A man walked over to him. He was a relative of the man whose ear Peter had cut off. "Didn't I see you with Him in the garden?"[3]

---

[2] Matthew 26:69-71

[3] John 18:26

Peter felt his life was in danger, so he denied it again with cursing. As the words fell from his lips, a rooster crowed again. He turned and saw Jesus looking straight at him. Peter hid his face in shame and ran away, just like the other disciples. They lacked the courage to stand up for Jesus in the face of death.

Jesus went to the cross, and the only disciple to stay close was John. The others might have stolen a glance from a distance, but John was there with Jesus. As Jesus breathed His last between two thieves, He looked down and saw His mother, Mary, next to John. He told John to look after his mother in His place. Church tradition says John did just that. Some think Mary might even have traveled with John to Ephesus, where he ministered later in life.

But for now, the disciples stayed in hiding, confused, and afraid, wondering what would happen to Jesus and them. But if they had paid attention and understood Jesus' words, they would have known.

Chapter 6
THE RESURRECTION

The time spent with Jesus was pivotal in shaping the disciples. Still, nothing would impact them more than the crucifixion and resurrection.

The way Jesus died is incredible. While Jesus hung on the cross, it became dark as night, even though it was the middle of the day. The moment He died, a massive earthquake hit Jerusalem, the thick curtain in the temple ripped in two. There were even sightings of godly people who had died wandering the city.

The soldiers who stood at the foot of the cross were in awe at everything that had happened. One of them even confessed, "This man really was God's Son!"[1]

It was a difficult time for the disciples. They hid and wondered what would happen to them. Would they go back to the lives they had before they met Jesus? Or would the religious leaders hunt them down and kill them? Would they need to escape to a foreign country? None expected what was about to happen even though Jesus had told them about it.

Three days later, most of them were in a room together, still afraid and hiding, when a woman who followed Jesus came barging in. She said she had been to the tomb and Jesus' body was gone. She said He had risen from the dead!

The disciples looked at each other. What was this crazy woman talking about? They didn't believe her. But she kept insisting Jesus had risen.

---

[1] Matthew 27:54

Peter and John jumped up and ran to the grave. Could it be true? They wanted to believe, but it seemed impossible. As they got closer, they noticed someone had moved the stone that covered the opening. John stopped when he reached the entrance, but Peter ran inside. The tomb was empty except for the burial cloth.

Later, Jesus appeared to the disciples. He scolded them for not believing. He even ate a meal with them. Then He disappeared.

One disciple wasn't with them when Jesus appeared. All the disciples excitedly told Thomas about their encounter, but he didn't believe it. He said, "If I don't see the mark of the nails, and put my hand into His side, I will never believe!"[2]

Later Jesus appeared again with Thomas in the room. Jesus asked Thomas to touch His hands and His side. Most people remember Thomas for doubting, but from that moment onward, He never doubts again. He will boldly

---

[2] John 20:25

stand for Jesus in the coming years, even give up His life for Him.

Peter was excited that Jesus was alive, but he wondered if He would accept him. After all, he denied Him three times. Will Jesus still want Him for a disciple? One day Peter told the others he is going fishing. Maybe he's questioning if he needs to get back to his old life. A few disciples decided to join him. They fished all night but caught nothing.

As the sun rises, they saw a man standing on the shore. He called out to them, "Men… You don't have any fish, do you?"

"No," they yell back.

"Cast the net on the right side of the boat, and you'll find some."

They throw their net and find it so full of fish they can't bring it in.

John looked at Peter, they must have both realized who it was, but John said, "It is the Lord!"[3]

---

[3] John 21:7

Peter jumped in the water and ran to Jesus. He's uncertain Jesus will want anything to do with him. But just like the story of the Prodigal Son, Jesus is there to receive him. He asks Peter three times if he loves Him. Each time Peter tells Jesus he does. Just like Peter denied Jesus three times, Jesus is giving Him three times to declare His love.

Jesus tells Peter two things as they walk the shore. First He said to him that when Peter is older, someone will take him by the hand and lead him where he doesn't want to go. Jesus was saying that one day Peter would die because of Jesus. Peter might have denied Jesus, but he would get another chance to face death for Him.

The next thing Jesus tells him is, "Follow me." Just like the beginning of their relationship, Jesus again asks Peter to be His disciple. Even though Peter had failed, even though he knew life with Jesus would end in certain death, Jesus was asking Peter to follow Him. Peter's heart raced, tears flowed down his cheeks in rivers. Those two words meant everything. Jesus had forgiven him, and he would follow Him for the rest of his life.

Chapter 7
ACTS OF THE APOSTLES

Before Jesus ascended into heaven, He left instructions for the disciples. "Go, therefore, and make disciples of all nations, baptizing them in the name of the Father and of the Son and of the Holy Spirit, teaching them to observe everything I have commanded you. And remember, I am with you always, to the end of the age."[1]

We call this, 'The Great Commission,' Because Jesus commissioned His disciples. From now on, they would be called Apostles.

---

[1] Matthew 28:19-20

> ## *Pentecost*
>
> *The day the Holy Spirit came and filled the Apostles, and the others with them was a special Jewish holiday called Pentecost. It has several other names, including: 'Feast of Harvest,' 'The Feast of Weeks', and 'The day of First Fruits.' This holiday takes place seven weeks after Passover. Jewish people call this day 'Shavout,' which is Hebrew for 'weeks.'*
>
> *Pentecost is the day that God gave Moses the Ten Commandments, so the day is also called, 'The Day of Giving of the Law.'*
>
> *As Christians, we celebrate Pentecost as the day God gave us His Holy Spirit.*

But before they could go to the entire world, Jesus gave them one more instruction. He told them they would have to wait in Jerusalem because He would send them the Holy Spirit to help them.

They must have wondered about this, but they waited for ten days. It was during that time that Peter stood up and spoke about Judas. Peter thought they should replace him and choose someone to take his place as the twelfth Apostle. Everyone thought this was a good idea, so they picked two men: Joseph, also called Barsabbas and Matthias. They cast lots to decide which of these men should have the honor. Casting lots might be like drawing straws today. The man chosen was Matthias.

Finally, the day of Pentecost came. It was during this particular Jewish holiday that something incredible happened. A group of about 120 people had gathered to pray. They were together in a room, praying and waiting. Even though they had closed the windows and doors, a mighty wind swept through the room.

They could feel and hear the wind blowing, it was tossing their hair around, but where was it coming from? Suddenly fire appeared on each of them. It looked like they were on fire but not burning. Then they all spoke in a language they did not understand.

A crowd gathered outside the house because of all the noise. There were Jewish men and women from all over the world in

Jerusalem for Passover. They spoke the languages of the lands where they lived.

The Apostles came outside still speaking in these strange languages, and the people heard them speaking in their own tongues, giving praise to God. Some people laughed at them because they thought they had been drinking too much wine.

Peter addressed the crowd. He explained what was happing and told them what they were witnessing was the gift of the Holy Spirit. Then he told them about Jesus. He said even though they had crucified Jesus, God had raised Him to life. Peter told them, "God has made this Jesus, whom you crucified, both Lord and Messiah!"[2]

The change in Peter is fantastic. Before he was afraid and denied even knowing Jesus, but after the Holy Spirit came on him, he boldly preached to the crowds.

When the people heard his message, they believed. That day 3,000 people turned to

---

[2] Acts 2:36

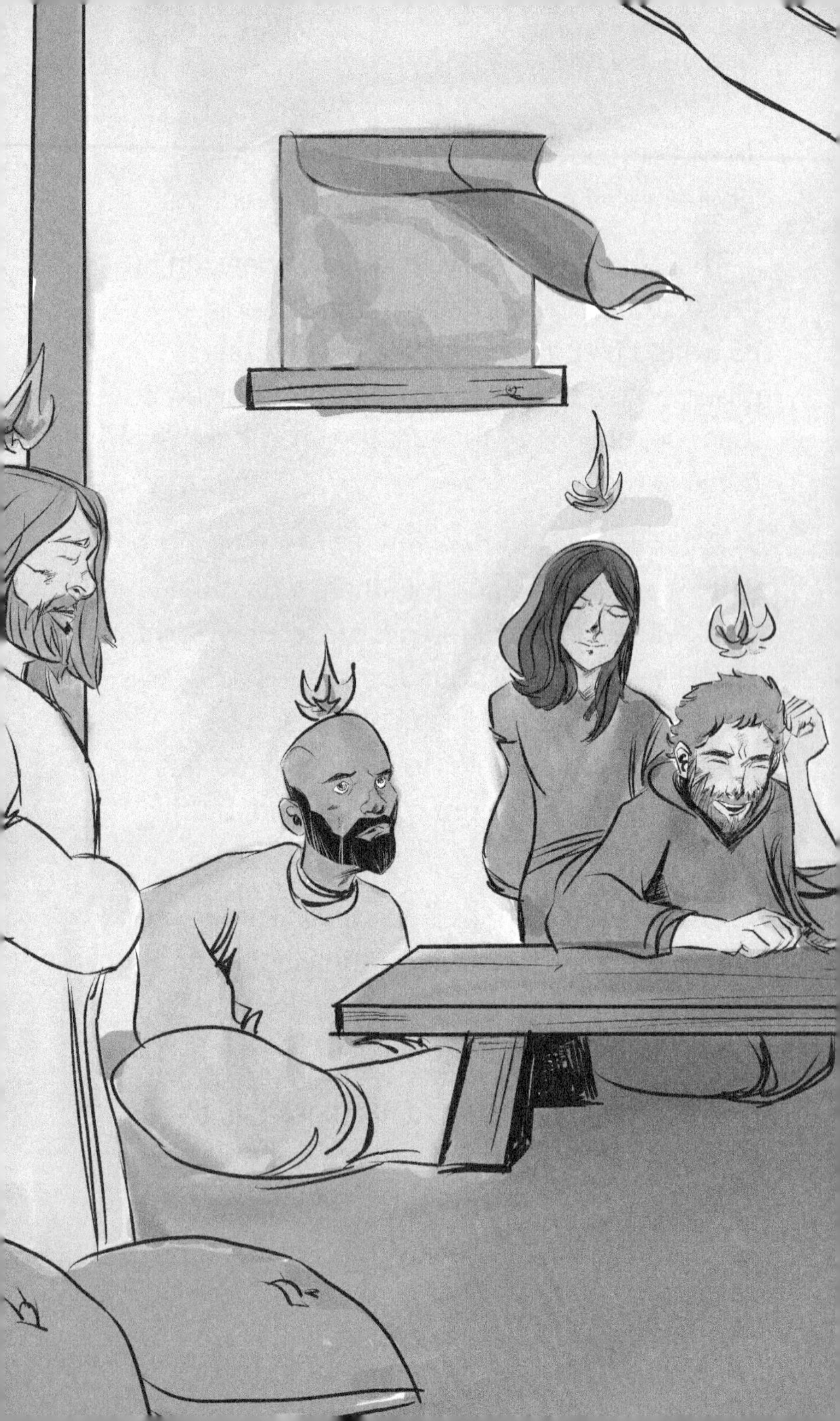

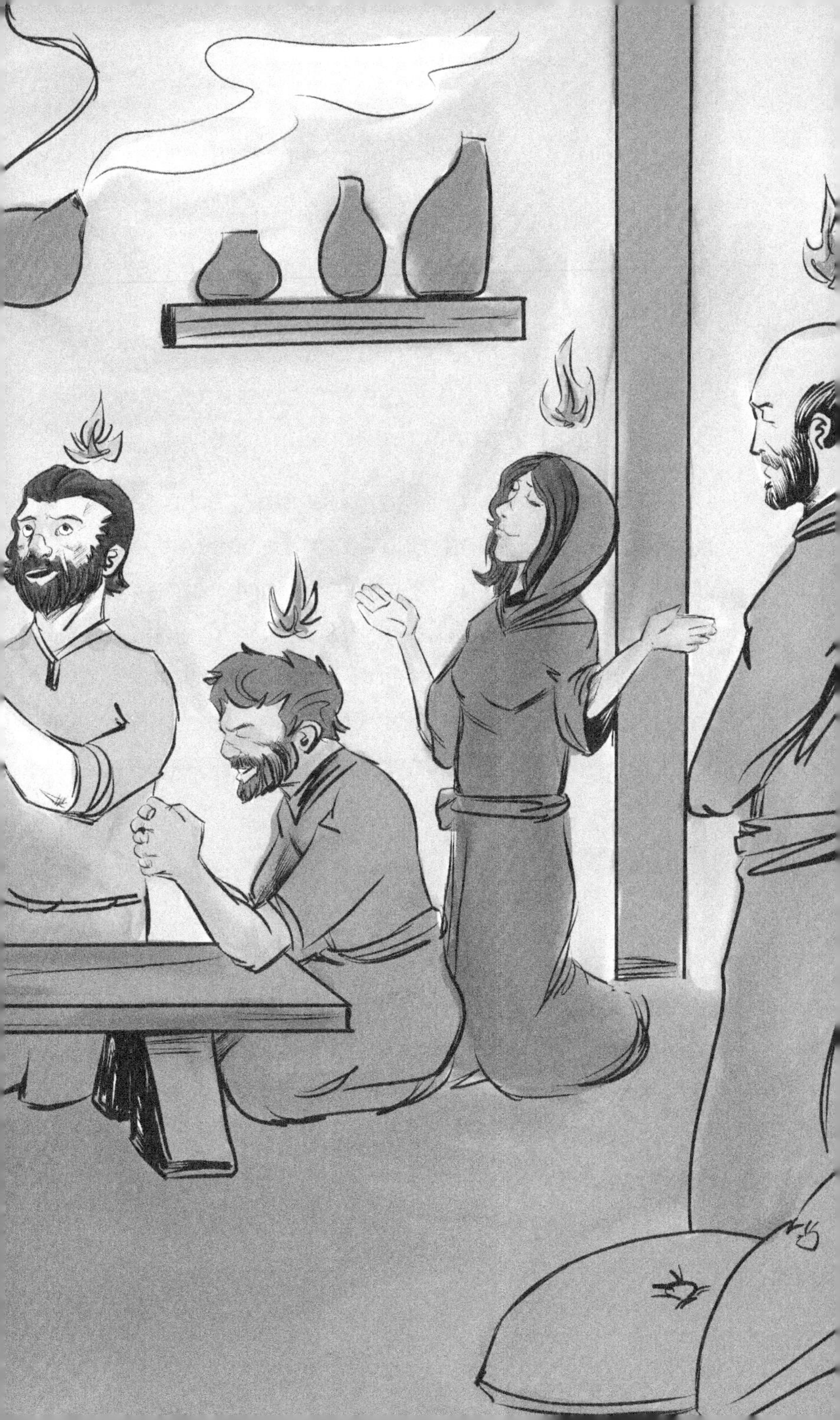

Jesus. But it was only the beginning.

The religious leaders were frantic. They assumed they had stopped Jesus, but now His disciples were turning the city upside down preaching He was alive. They tried to stop them, they had them arrested and beaten, but they only preached more.

Everyone in Jerusalem was amazed and respected the Apostles. When Peter walked down the street, sick people would come and sit so that his shadow would fall on them, and they would receive healing. God was doing incredible things through His Apostles, but so far only among the Jewish people. But that was about to change.

A Man Named Cornelius

One day Peter was relaxing on a quiet rooftop when he saw a vision. A vision is like a dream that happens when someone is awake. In his vision he saw a group of unclean animals that Jewish people couldn't eat because they weren't kosher. Jewish people had been given commandments by God on which foods they were allowed to eat.

The Kosher Law

Kosher refers to the laws about what foods Jews are permitted to eat. Still today, Jewish people observe the kosher laws.

In Leviticus 11, God gives Moses the rules for what foods are clean and what are unclean. God told them they could only eat animals with split hooves that chewed their cud. For example, a cow has split hooves and chews its cud, so it is kosher, but a pig even though it has split hooves does not chew its cud, so it's not kosher. They also had to be sure there was no blood in the meat they ate. Fish had to have scales, or they were unclean. So no eating catfish or sharks!. They could some eat birds, but God told them which ones they couldn't eat, like eagles or vultures. But believe it or not, some insects are kosher. John the Baptist ate locust, which was kosher.

For people keeping kosher, they must keep milk separate from the meat. If you want ice cream after your meal, you have to wait for a while.

A voice spoke to Peter, "Get up, Peter; kill and eat!"

He thought it must be a test. He told the Lord he had never eaten anything unclean.

God told him. "What God has made clean, you must not call common."[3]

That happened three times, then the vision vanished. As he thought about the vision, men arrived and announced they were looking for Peter. They said they worked for a Roman Centurion named Cornelius. He had seen an angel who told him to find Peter and bring him to his house.

Peter followed them to Caesarea. When he entered Cornelius' house, he found it full of people. Cornelius had called all of his relatives and friends and told them about the angel he had seen, and he invited them to come to listen to Peter.

Jewish law said Peter couldn't go inside the house of a Gentile. But Peter realized God didn't want him to look down on anyone. So

---

[3] Acts 10:15

Peter went inside and told the people about Jesus.

Before he had finished his sermon, the Holy Spirit came down on them. Peter now understood, Jesus was for everyone, not only for the Jewish people. From there, the Gospel continued to spread.

James Beheaded

Not long after that, King Herod began to persecute the church. He had many Christians arrested, including the Apostle James, the brother of John.

Herod knew James was an influential leader, so he targeted him to discourage the church. He hoped if he executed James, then the church would fall apart. So he took James and had him killed.

According to one of the early church writers, as the guard led him to his execution, James showed such courage that the guard became a Christian too. That man chose to die next to James.

The Family of Herod

Several people ruled during the time of the Apostles that belonged to the same family called Herod.

The Roman government appointed Herod the Great to rule the area of Israel. He was the ruler during the time of Jesus' birth. The Jews didn't like him because he wasn't Jewish, but he won them over by rebuilding the temple. The group of Jews who became loyal to him were called Herodians. When the wise men came to inquire about the birth of Jesus, Herod told them to report back to him. He planned to have Jesus killed. When they didn't tell him, Herod ordered all the baby boys in Bethlehem under two years old killed.

After Herod the Great died, his four sons divided his kingdom among them. One of his sons was named Herod Antipas. He was the Herod who imprisoned John the Baptist and ordered his execution. He also had a brief meeting with Jesus. He wondered if Jesus might have been John, raised from the dead.

Herod Agrippa, I was a grandson of Herod the Great. When all of Herod's sons died, they gave him the entire area to rule. It was this Herod who had James killed, and Peter put in prison. One day as he gave a speech, the people chanted he was a god. Because he didn't give God the glory, an angel struck him dead. (See Acts 12)

His son, Herod Agrippa II, took over as a teenager and became the last of the Herod line. He was called King Agrippa and was the one who heard Paul speak in Acts 25.

The Jewish leaders were glad James had died. They encouraged Herod to keep going after the church. Next, he set his sights on Peter and had him arrested.

But the church got together and prayed for him. At midnight, as Peter slept, an angel came and woke him. The chains on his wrists fell off. The angel told him to put on his coat and follow him.

Peter glanced at the guards sleeping next to him as he quietly stood and followed the angel to the main gates. The massive doors would be impossible to open. But as they approached, the gates flung open on their own. He rubbed his eyes. It seemed like a dream. Then the angel disappeared.

Peter escaped, and He and the Apostles continued preaching about Jesus, despite persecution. Soon they would carry the Gospel into distant lands.

Chapter 8
THE UTTERMOST PARTS OF THE EARTH

What happened to the Apostles after the book of Acts? Most of what we know comes from tradition and church history. Sometimes it's hard to separate actual history from the legends. Even in the legends, there might be elements of truth that give us insight into who these men were and what they did.

What we know for sure is that all the Apostles continued to preach throughout their lives. Of the original twelve, Judas Iscariot was dead, but Matthias had taken his place. Herod had killed James, so that left eleven. Here is a look at the remaining ten Apostles, where they traveled, some of their legends, and how they died.

Peter

Peter followed Jesus' call to be a 'fisher of men'. After the events of the Book of Acts, Peter traveled to many places preaching the Gospel and starting churches. He took a young man named Mark and trained him to continue the work. It was this young man who wrote the Gospel of Mark. The material for his Gospel came straight from Peter's stories.

Peter wrote letters to the churches in different towns where he ministered. The New Testament includes two of these letters. We call them First and Second Peter. In the first letter, he addresses people in different towns. These were probably some places where he traveled. He also spent time in Rome and started the church there.

Peter spent his last years in Rome. During that time, he must have remembered what Jesus told him about how he would die. Peter knew he would eventually give his life for the Gospel.

That day came when the head of the Roman Government, a man named Nero, increased his persecution of the church. He planned to have Peter arrested and executed. There is a story told by an early Christian writer about Peter's death.

In the story, the church at Rome finds out about Nero's plot and begs Peter to run. Peter is on his way out of the city when he sees Jesus walking entering. Peter stops and asks, "Lord, Where are you going?"

Jesus answers, "I'm going to be crucified again."

Peter realized that Jesus was telling him it was his time to die. Peter turned around and headed back. They arrested him, and some accounts say they also arrested his wife. First, they crucified his wife while Peter watched. "Remember Jesus," he encouraged her.

Then it was his turn. Peter felt unworthy to die on a cross as Jesus did. He requested that they crucify him upside down. Peter may have denied Jesus one night many years earlier, but he never did again. He preached and lived boldly for Jesus until his dying day.

Andrew

Peter's brother Andrew traveled to many places to preach the good news about Jesus. One place he visited was Scythia. It was a large area that included parts of modern-day Ukraine, Russia, and Poland. It was also very dangerous, but Andrew was a bold man and didn't shy away from danger. He did so much work in the area that today the people of Russia remember Andrew as the Apostle to their country.

Church history says Andrew also traveled to Greece, where he met a local governor named Aegeates, who strongly opposed the Christian faith. When the governor's wife accepted Jesus, he was so angry he had Andrew beaten and crucified on an 'X' shaped cross. This cross has come to be known as Saint Andrew's Cross.

When Andrew looked at the cross, he wasn't afraid, but instead, he wore a smile. It made him glad to know that he would die on a cross like his Savior. The governor wanted Andrew to suffer a slow death, and so he did not nail him to the cross but tied him up and did not break his legs. Because of this, it took several days for him to die.

People heard about how this godly man was suffering and crowded to see him. As he was hanging on the cross, he had a smile on his face and even laughed. Someone asked him why he would laugh when everyone around him was heartbroken. Andrew was full of joy because he would soon be with Jesus again. He told them the governor couldn't harm him. Heaven was waiting for him.

The people were horrified at the sight of Andrew's torture. They came to the governor and demanded he let him go. Aegeates came to see Andrew and considered setting him free. Still, Andrew demanded that no one release him and deny him the privilege of being crucified. Andrew passed from this world to the next full of the joy of the Lord. He

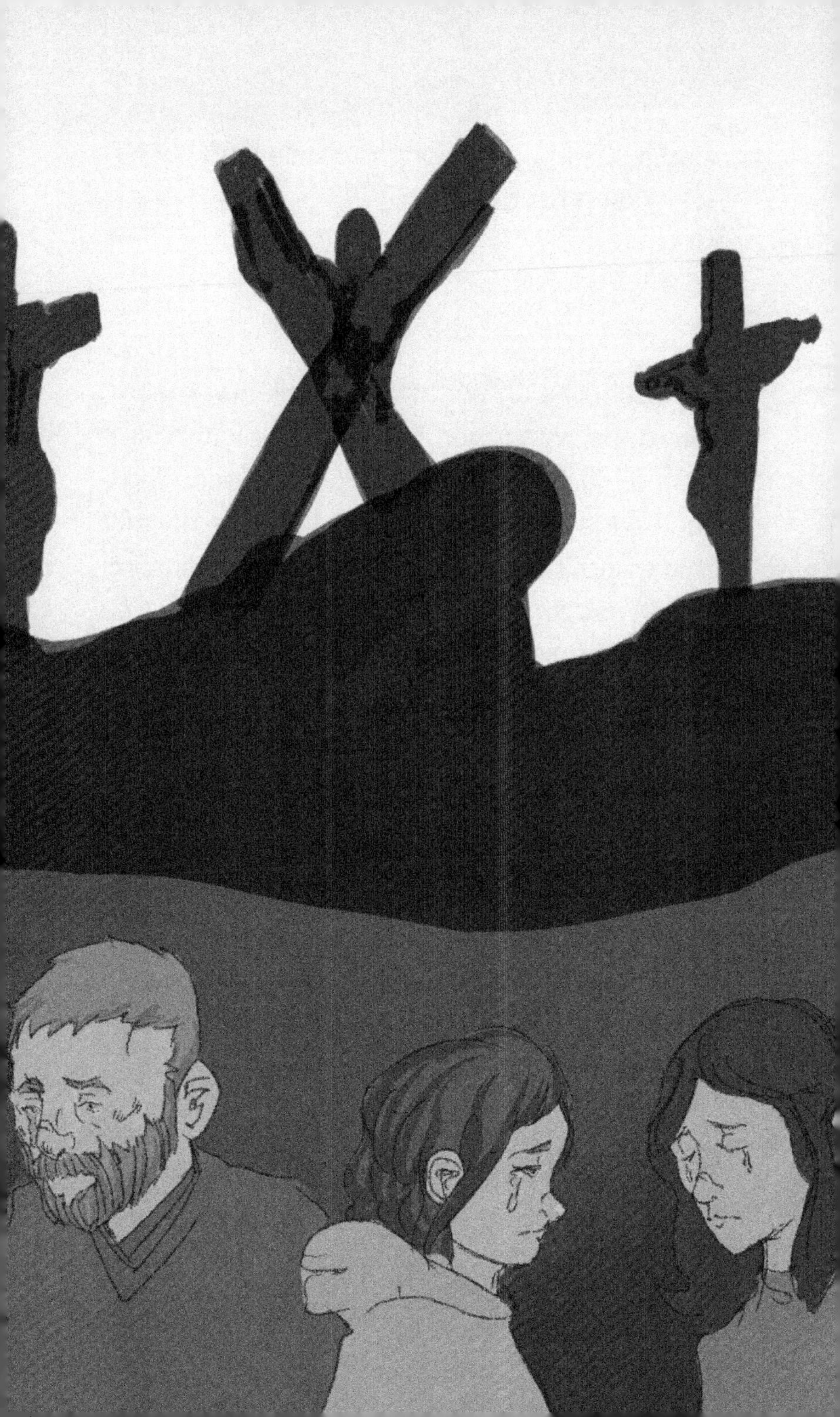

had a shining testimony to those who witnessed his death.

Matthew

Matthew's career as a tax collector made him good with a pen. It's easy to picture him as the official scribe of the group, recording the things Jesus said and did. Before he left this world, he recorded the story of Jesus into what we call, The Gospel of Matthew. The only other disciple to write a Gospel was John. Even though his people hated him before he met Jesus, Matthew became an admired Apostle.

In his Gospel, Matthew wanted to show that Jesus was the fulfillment of the Old Testament. There was a leader in the early church named Jerome, who said Matthew wrote his Gospel in Hebrew. He claims to have seen the original document and made a copy by hand.

Matthew's Gospel has traveled the world going places that Matthew could never have imagined. But he also traveled far from Jerusalem, carrying the Gospel of Jesus everywhere he went. He even preached in some dangerous places.

One legend says God commanded him to preach in a place called Myrna, where a group of cannibals lived. The cannibals tried to poison him, but the poison didn't hurt him at all. Matthew drove demons out of many of the people, but the king became angry with him and had executed.

What we know for sure is that Matthew traveled to many places preaching the Gospel. He preached in Persia, Macedonia, and Parthia and later Ethiopia. Tradition says his tormentors pinned him to the ground and beheaded him. He died around A.D. 60, about thirty years after the resurrection.

Philip

Most stories have Philip and Nathanael traveling together at least part of the time. When Jesus sent them out as part of their training, He always sent them in groups of two, so it's easy to imagine that they stuck together after the resurrection too.

These two Apostles traveled to India together. The people of India claim Philip translated the Gospel of Matthew in their language, but some people think it was Nathanael. Philip preached in many places, including Asia and Athens. He traveled to a city called Hierapolis, in modern Turkey, where a group of idol worshippers beat him and crucified him.

In 2011, archeologists uncovered a tomb in Hierapolis that they believe was Philip's burial place. His bones were taken out long ago and are now in Rome, along with several other Apostles.

Nathanael (also known as Bartholomew)

Not only did Nathanael travel with Philip, but he was probably with him when he died in Hierapolis. He founded a church in India and another one in Armenia. He finally gave His life for the Gospel in India. According to tradition, he died on September 11th. He died a painful death when evil men first beat him with clubs, then skinned him alive and beheaded him, all for preaching about Jesus.

Thomas

Most people remember Thomas because he doubted Jesus had risen, but he lived an extraordinarily bold life after Jesus appeared to him.

He traveled to Persia, Parthia, and India preaching the Gospel. There is an interesting legend about Thomas that tells how he came to India.

In the legend, Jesus appears to Thomas and tells him to go to India and preach. But Thomas refused. He pleads with the Lord. He offers to go anywhere but India. One day an Indian man came to Jerusalem looking to buy a slave to build a palace for a distant king. As he walks through the market, a man approaches and tells him he has a slave he would like to sell. He says the man is a skilled builder.

The man is very interested. He was looking for a craftsman and asked to see the slave. Just then, Thomas passed through the market. The man points at Thomas, "There he is."

Thomas looks up and sees Jesus. He discovers Jesus has sold him, and he is going to India. Thomas has no choice. He travels with the man to India and finds himself before a king.

The king orders Thomas to build a summer palace for him. Thomas assures him that he is a skilled builder and asks for money to get started. Thomas then takes the money and goes out to the countryside, where he gives the money to the poor and preaches the Gospel to them.

After a while, the king asks for a report on his building project. Thomas tells him it is going well, but he needs more money for the project. The king gives him the money, and Thomas again gives it all away.

One day the king asks to see the palace. "I have been building you the finest palace," Thomas tells him. "It is more beautiful than any palace you have ever seen on this earth. But you cannot see it. The palace is in heaven."

The king is furious and plans to execute Thomas. But when the king's brother has a near-death experience, he claims to have seen the heavenly palace. He tells the king he has seen the palace, and it is more beautiful than anything he could ever imagine.

While this is only a legend, it must show the boldness of Thomas and how much people thought of him.

Church history tells us that Thomas did, in fact, travel to India. Centuries later, when people from the west came to India, they heard stories from Christians of how the Apostle Thomas preached to them.

Some people were upset with Thomas and the Gospel he preached. It went against their traditions and the gods they served. One day men with spears attacked him, stabbed him, and threw him into a fire. His followers buried him in what is now Chennai, India. You can still visit his tomb today, inside the Santhome Cathedral.

James, the son of Alphaeus

We don't know much about James, the brother of Matthew. Some people think before he met Jesus, he was also a tax collector like his brother. Some believe he was a member of the Zealots like Simon. Some stories say James traveled to Persia and preached there before they crucified him. Another story says he was sawed in two. Even though we don't know much about him, what we know is, like the rest of the Apostles, he preached and died for his faith.

Simon, the Zealot

Simon used to belong to the group of Zealots, but now he had a different mission in life. Stories claim he traveled to Egypt and down into Africa and as far west as England. His traveling partner, for some of his journeys, was Thaddaeus.

In one story, both he and Thaddaeus present the Gospel to a king. The king had two sorcerers that worked for him. These two magicians encountered the real power of God. The king believed the Apostles and had the magicians put in prison to wait for their execution. But the Apostles begged the king to spare the men.

Instead of being grateful that the Apostles saved them from execution, the sorcerers became enraged at Simon and Thaddaeus. The magicians followed them from town to town, mocking and criticizing them all over Persia. But even with the opposition, people believed the message of salvation and were coming to Christ everywhere they traveled. In one town, the magicians found a group of priests at a pagan temple. They stirred up the priest, and together they grabbed the Apostles and beat them with clubs while others threw stones.

According to the story, the King of Persia buried their bodies in the capital city inside a new church he had built.

***Thaddeus** (also called **Judas**)*

There is an interesting legend about Thaddeus that says a king from a place called Edessa, in modern Turkey, heard the news about Jesus and believed in Him.

This king, named Abgarus, sent letters to Jesus, asking Him to come to his city. The legend says Jesus sent a letter back and told him he could not come because God had only sent Him to Israel. But Jesus replied that He would send one of His disciples after His resurrection.

Some time after the day of Pentecost, the story says, that the Apostles elected Thaddeus to go preach to King Abgarus. The king believed in Jesus and asked Thaddeus to preach to the people in his country.

While we can't be sure if there is any truth to this legend, one early church father, Jerome, seemed to think Thaddaeus had gone to Edessa. There were even copies of the letter supposedly written by Jesus found engraved in homes hundreds of miles from Edessa.

There are two different accounts of how Thaddeus died, so we can't be sure which one is accurate. One report says he died when he traveled to Ararat, where men shot him with arrows, but other accounts link him with Simon the Zealot. He could have been with Simon when he died, escaped, and continued to travel and preach, finally arriving in Ararat.

Matthias

Matthias was the last to be added to the group of disciples when he took Judas' place. His name means "gift of God." It's a similar name to Matthew. Jesus didn't choose him to be one of the twelve, and some people think Paul was the actual replacement Jesus chose. But we know Matthias had been with the disciples from the time of Jesus' baptism and saw Him ascend into heaven. He was probably one of the seventy disciples sent out to preach and perform miracles.

Some sources claim he began to travel with Peter and Andrew. In one of these cities, he was locked in prison, but a miracle set him free. Another time someone tried to poison him, but the poison didn't hurt him at all.

There is some debate about his death. Some think he was sentenced to death by Ananias, the High Priest who had Jesus arrested. They believe Ananias had him stoned. Others believe his death happened in a place called Colchis, in the modern country of Georgia. No matter where he died, we can be sure he spent his life like the other disciples, preaching the name of Jesus.

John

The Apostle John wrote five books of the New Testament. In his Gospel, he refers to himself as the 'disciple that Jesus loved.' It amazed John that Jesus loved him so much, and he wanted to communicate that love to us. He also wrote three letters we call *First, Second, and Third John*. We call his final letter, *Revelation*. It records the vision he had about the end times.

John opens the book of Revelation by saying he is on the Island of Patmos because of the word of God. Patmos was an island where the Romans sent prisoners and forced them to endure hard labor. John says he was there as punishment for preaching the Word of God.

Church history tells us before the Romans sent him to Patmos, they had sentenced him

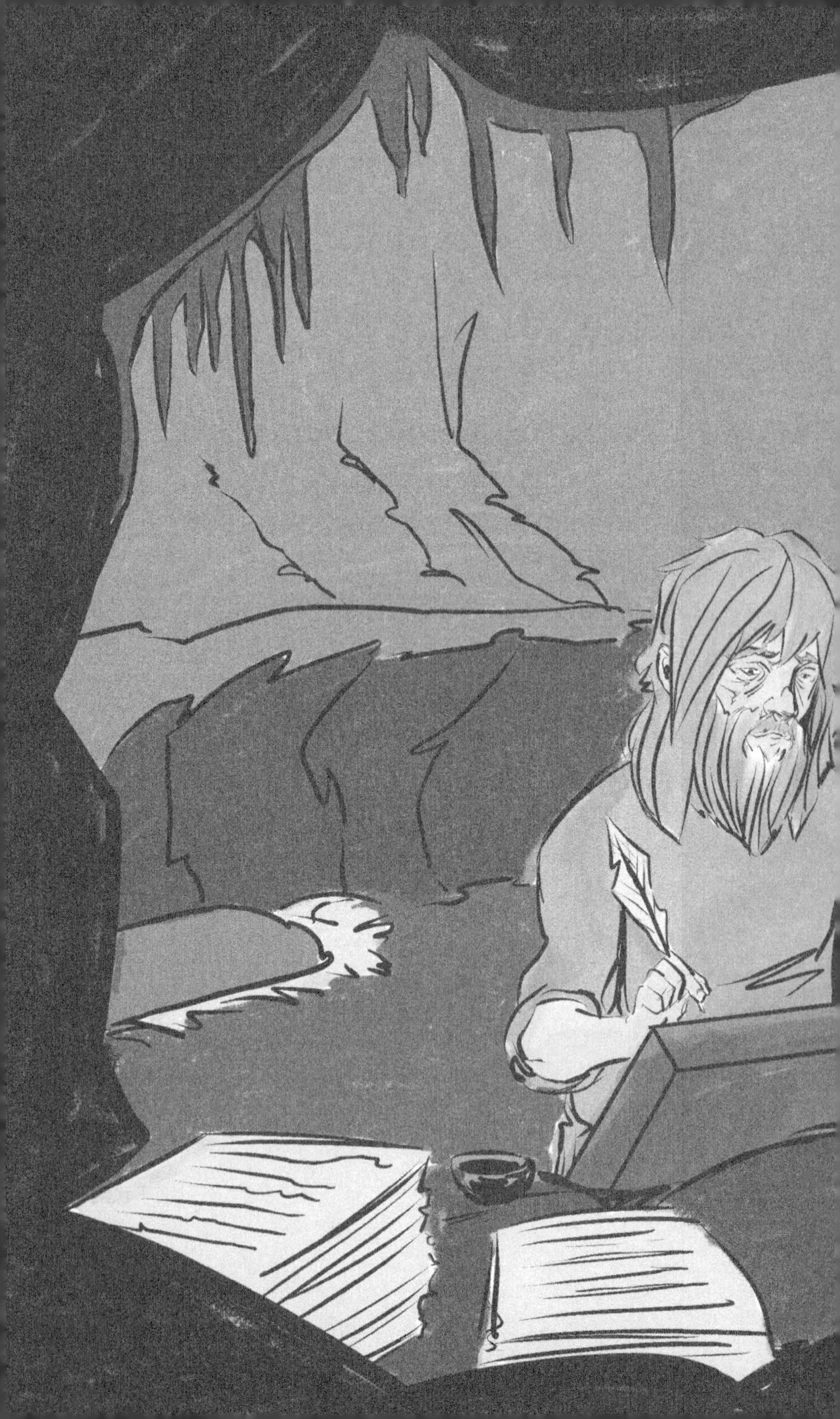

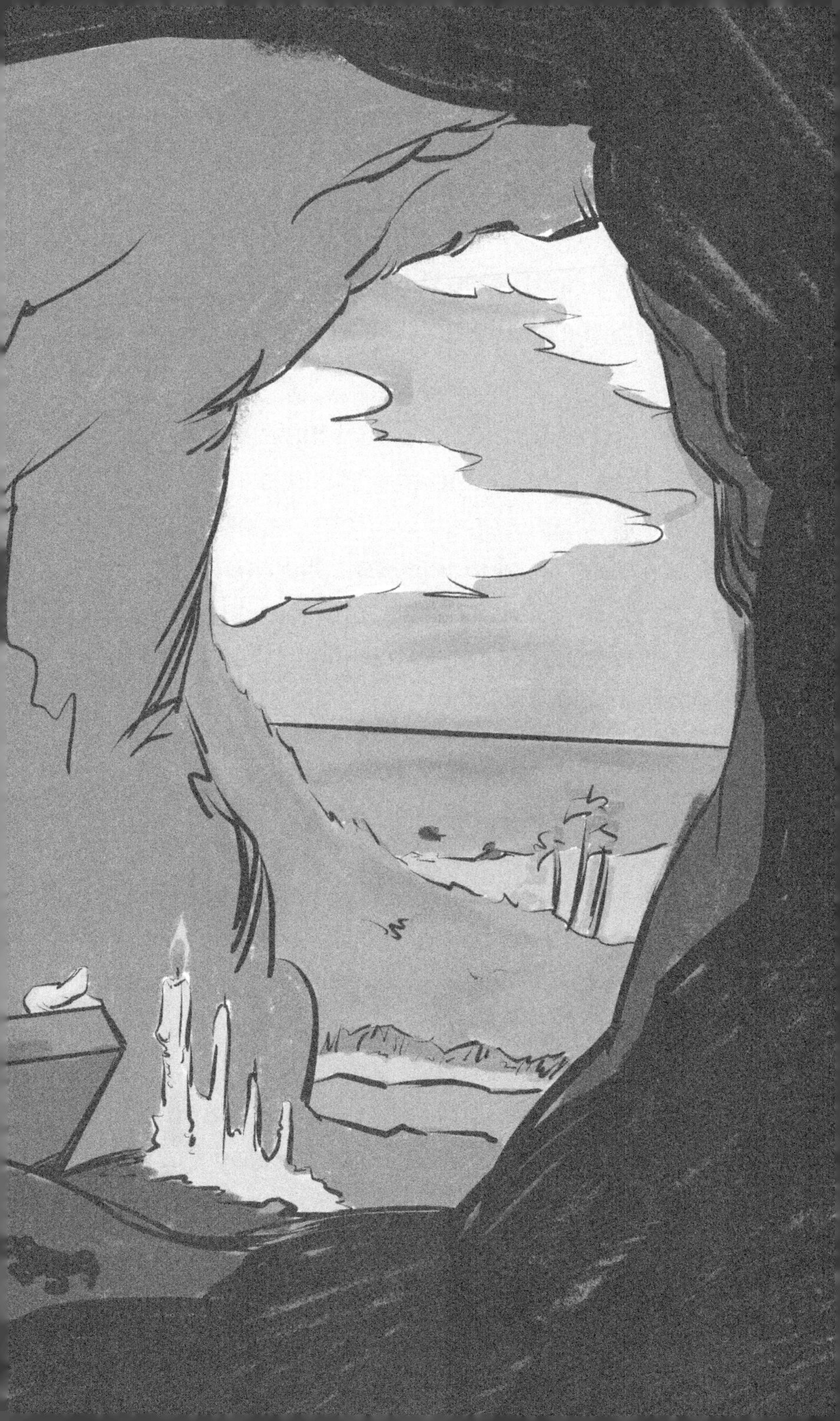

to execution. One form of execution involved throwing people into vats of boiling oil. It was a painful way to die. John probably watched others die in the oil. When his turn came, they threw him into the oil, but it didn't burn him at all.

When his tormenters saw the oil didn't kill him, they sent him to the prison camp at Patmos. John stayed on Patmos for many years before being released. He wrote the book of Revelation there, inside a cave. He traveled and preached in many cities in his lifetime. One city he spent a lot of time at is Ephesus.

John outlived all the other Apostles. There was a story about John when he was older and living in Ephesus. A young man had become a Christian, and John asked the pastor of the church there to take care of him and train him. He then spent several years traveling to other towns for ministry. When he returned, he searched for the man, but the pastor informed him the man had left the church.

John scolded the pastor for not taking better care to disciple the man. He set off looking for him to bring him back. He discovered the man had become the leader of a dangerous gang of thieves. John walked into an area where the gang worked and let them capture him. He demanded to see their leader.

The gang brought John to the young man. When the man saw John, he wept. He said he felt unworthy to come back to Jesus. John convinced him that God still loved him and brought him back, and eventually, he became a leader of the church.

This story gives us an idea of the kind of man John was. He was a man full of the love of God and willing to lay down his life for the Gospel. John lived to a ripe old age. At the end of his life, it was hard for him to walk, so men carried him to church. When he could hardly speak anymore, he would tell the church, "Children, love one another." He was the only disciple who died of natural causes. He died around A.D. 98.

The Apostles had been with Jesus, and it changed them. They became filled with a passion for telling the world that Jesus was alive, and because He was alive, they could live too. They weren't afraid of what people could do to them in this life because they knew they would live forever because of their faith in Jesus. They traveled the known world preaching about Jesus, and their testimony is still speaking to us today.

Prayer

If you want to follow the Disciples example and make Jesus Christ your Lord and Savior you can ask Him to come into your life by praying a prayer like this:

Lord Jesus, I believe in you and I believe you came and died to save me and I believe you are risen from the dead. I ask you to save me and forgive me for my sin and wrong things I've done. Come into my life and make me a new person. Thank you for your gift of salvation. Amen.

Bibliography

Zondervan Handbook to the Bible (Grand Rapids, MI: Zondervan Publishing House, 1999)

William Barclay, The Master's Men, (Nashville, TN. Abingdon Press, 1959)

Ruth Specter Lascelle , Jewish Faith and The New Covenant, Revised Edition (Van Nuys, CA: Rock of Israel Ministries)

John Foxe, The New Foxes Book of Martyrs, updated by Harold J. Chadwick (North Brunswick, NJ: Bridge-Logos Publishers, 1997)

Ronald Brownrigg, The Twelve Apostles (New York, NY: Macmillan Publishing Co, Inc, 1974)

Burial site of Philip:

https://www.biblicalarchaeology.org/daily/biblical-sites-places/biblical-archaeology-sites/tomb-of-apostle-philip-found/ (accessed 01/09/2020)

https://www.oca.org/saints/lives/2015/08/09/102243-apostle-matthias-of-the-seventy (accessed 01/09/2020) https://overviewbible.com/matthias-the-apostle/ (accessed 01/09/2020)

(Author is not responsible for the above websites)

Printed in Great Britain
by Amazon